THIS BOOK BELONGS TO:

_____

THE POETRY
OF
WILDFLOWERS

FIELD JOURNAL

Rose

The POETRY

of Wildflowers

FIELD JOURNAL

For the Traveler

compiled and edited by

R. CLIFT

WITH ORIGINAL ILLUSTRATIONS BY

THE "RAPHAEL OF FLOWERS"

PIERRE–JOSEPH REDOUTÉ

AND

OTHER 19TH CENTURY ARTISTS

VOL. I.

NEW YORK
1849

*To my grandmother, Sandra, thank you
for teaching me how to love unconditionally.*

I'd rather be a wildflower— overlooked, underestimated, maybe even a little forgotten. Untamed and free to live and grow wherever I please. Yes, maybe a garden flower is more proper and pretty with no torn petals or missing leaves like me, but that perfect rose can only ever depend on another for nurturing, and hope to be admired where it is planted— but believe me when I say, people are neglectful things, and you must learn to nuture yourself. You must learn to be wild. When the winter frosts have come and gone— we {the wild ones} will be the ones strong enough, on our own, to bloom. R. CLIFT.

INTRODUCTION.

Words are symphonies— they each attach themselves to a kaleidoscope of memories. When a single word is read, every memory that is associated with that word comes flooding in— whether we realize it or not. Promise. Separation. Romance. Courage. In our lives, we have experienced countless moments that attach themselves to words such as these— like a note is a part of a grand orchestra, a single memory is a part of all that is you.

I created this book to unravel orchestras into notes, to unravel you into the singular moments that you are made of— to find the poetry buried deep within them. To encourage that poetry to push through the dark, to reach toward the light, to grow, to bloom.

Now, I must take a moment to tell you about a time when flowers had their own language, which serves as the cornerstone of this poetry prompt journal. In the 19th century, the first western flower dictionary called 'Le Langage des Fleurs' was compiled by Madame Charlotte de Latour in 1819.
'The Language of Flowers' was quickly translated into english and would go on to become a phenomenon in Victorian high society.

In these Victorian times, showing open displays of emotion was a complicated ordeal due to society's strict protocol-- so this coded language of flowers became the clandestine method of sending a secret message to a friend, lover, or even to an enemy.

Individual flowers have their own meanings-- Rosemary for remembrance, Bluebell for sorrowful regret, a White Rose to say 'I am worthy of you'--the list goes on and on into the hundreds.

When put together, in carefully crafted bouquets-- they were able to send full and expressive messages to one another. For example, one would send Everlasting Pea (Meet me), Night Convolvulus (To-night), and Forget-me-not flowers (Do not forget)-- to convey the message: "Meet me tonight; do not forget."

It is important to note that flowers occasionally had different or multiple meanings depending on location, time, and the context of what other flowers they were paired with.

Young women often wore blooms in their hair, tucked into a bodice, or on their evening gowns. Many would carry a small flower arrangement known as a nosegay, posy, or tussie-mussie to convey these coded messages of affection, grief, or desire. Whether worn or carried, these flowers allowed Victorians to express their true feelings in a cryptic and alluring way.

I find studying the history of the language of flowers absolutely fascinating— as well as reading the old poetry often found in the same books and realizing poets haven't really changed all that much in the past two hundred years.

We are still yearning, still searching for love, still enduring grief, still hoping for the moon and stars to notice us.

It is a privilege to learn where these Victorian meanings originate from (many are old legends & folklore). I imagine how they could've been used to send specific messages, how maybe I could use them today to express how I feel.

It's even more special knowing that this method of communicating with flowers only lasted a short while in a notoriously ephemeral period in history— but what an extraordinary time it was— to speak out in flowers and the ones you love most would understand exactly what you were trying to say, in a time when emotion was intense, but rarely able to be expressed aloud.

I hope these select pages, and the included complete Victorian Flower Dictionary will encourage you to look at flowers in a new way, and to write endless poetry based on whichever sentiments and meanings inspire you most.

In the time it took to write and compile this book, I have come to realize--- I've been looking at flowers all my life and until now, I never really saw them, I never really cared to learn their names or their significance--- but now--- whenever I walk into a flower shop or plant nursery, an open field or even a giant park--- I am surrounded by familiar friends, excited to point them out and say hello--- and as they blossom around me, I am immersed in a garden of true meaning.

R. Clift

How to
Use
This Book

Dear Poet,

With these Victorian meanings of flowers as your own poetry prompts— all I ask is that you may allow your heart and mind to wander freely.

Remember, this poetry isn't meant to be perfect. It isn't meant to be achingly forced or agonized over— it is meant to be a release, an expression, a chance for growth— it is meant to lead you to the parts of yourself that need the most care.

I want this book to be whatever you need it to be— as an artist looking for a place to be authentic. So please, my darling, let your ink dance across these lines with beautiful abandon, and with the wonder of nature & human emotion as the enriched soil where your words are planted— may poetry bloom.

Ever yours,
xx Rachel

CONTENTS.

Camellia. Narcissus & Pansy

PREFACE.

Are not flowers the earliest gift of love?
Do they not, mutely eloquent, oft speak
For absent or for trembling hearts, and bear
Kisses and sighs on their perfumed lips,
And worlds of thoughts and fancies in their tears,
Touched by the rainbow's dyes? Have ye ne'er
      prized
Some token flower— an early rose— a bunch
Of young Spring's first and sweetest violets,
      culled
And given into yours by hands so dear,
That all flowers seemed grown holier from that
      time?
Have you ne'er *hoarded* such a simple gift,
Ay, through long years, e'en when each shrunken
      leaf
Bore not a semblance to the thing it was,
And the soft fragrance, that had once been there,
Had changed from sweet to noisome,— and e'en
      then,
For very fondness, could not fling away
Those dim and faded records of past,
But laid the frail things in their wonted place,
To gaze, and dream, and weep upon again?

                The Bouquet, L. A. TWAMLEY, 1846.

AMARYLLIS

Determination & Worth Beyond Beauty

Amaryllis brasiliensis

P.J.Redouté

Victor sculp.

Determination

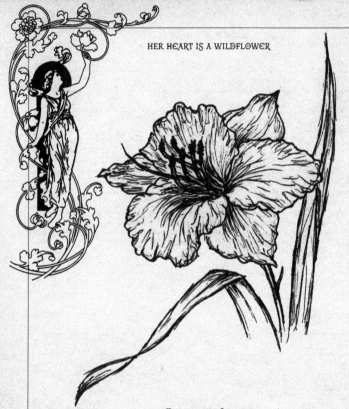

AMARYLLIS

R. Clift

Amaryllis brasiliensis

R. CLIFT

Her heart weaves through Amaryllis, tending to the love she plants daily in her chest. Radiance of her own making. Breathing in sunlight. Exhaling truth like a whisper of the wind.

She loses herself all too often, aching to find her true place. She surrounds herself in towering trees. Here— a sense of belonging. The forest is her sanctuary. Where she can bloom and become. Where she can adore all who stumble in and out of her life.

The stars gaze as she dances with the night. An illustrious being. Free of regret. Free of shadow. The burning lights throw themselves from the sky for a chance at landing in the palm of her hand.

Her arms outstretched to the moon. The tides search for her on every coast. Flames reflect in her burnished brown eyes. Release and reverie.

Leaves fall around her like a veil being dropped. There is a kind of magic within her that has never been fully understood, passed through generations of wild, willful, wondrous women— and this, whether she believes it or not, begs the conclusion that the universe itself can only ever be complete with her in it.

ANEMONE

Forsaken

Anemone vernalis

Forsaken

APPLE BLOSSOM

Knowledge & Illumination

Malus domestica

P. J. Redouté

Chapuy sculp.

Illumination

ASTER

Afterthought

Callistephus chinensis

P.J. Redouté

Bessin sculp.

Afterthought

_____
_____
_____
_____
_____
_____
_____
_____
_____
_____
_____
_____
_____
_____
_____
_____
_____
_____
_____
_____
_____
_____
_____
_____
_____

AZALEA

Take care of yourself for me

Rhododendron

P. J. Redouté

Lambert jeune sculp.

Take care of yourself for me

BASIL

Hatred

Ocimum grandiflorum

P. J. Redouté

Fr. Hulbert sculp.

Hatred

BELLFLOWER

Gratitude

Campanula

G. Van Spaendonck   P. J. Le Grand. sculp.

Gratitude

_____
_____
_____
_____
_____
_____
_____
_____
_____
_____
_____
_____
_____
_____
_____
_____
_____
_____
_____
_____
_____
_____
_____
_____
_____

BIRD OF PARADISE .

Magnificence

Strelitzia reginae

P. J. Redouté

Liliacées

Magnificence

HER HEART IS A WILDFLOWER

BIRD OF PARADISE

R. Clift   *Strelitzia reginae*

R. CLIFT

Her heart unfurls its wings like bird of paradise blooming. Feathers of devotion. She offers sanctuary, keeping wounded hearts safe between her ribs. A place to rest beneath her wings.

She has always seen the beauty in dying things, fallen leaves, endings, rainy mornings. Still her copper eyes search for more. Dawn til dusk. Golden light weaving through mountaintops. Darkness settling in the valley.

She believes everyone, everything, every moment of this life should know infinite love. If no one else, she will be the one to give it to them. Until her very last breath.

She will never cease, for she longs to be the kind of woman, the kind of human, that makes others feel worthwhile. From the day of her own birth to the day she finds the one to the day her children walk the earth to the day they all grow old to the day the stars burn out, she will follow in the footsteps of unconditional love, wings unfolded, ever searching for hearts to save.

BLOODROOT

Strength & Protective Love

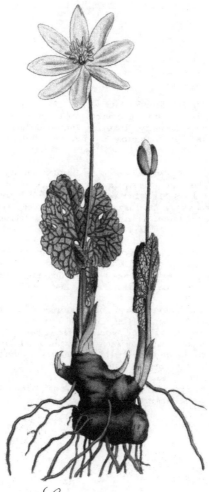

Sanguinaria canadensis

S.T.Edwards

W.Curtis sculp.

Protective Love

BLUEBELL

Constancy & Sorrowful Regret

Hyacinthoides non-scripta

Sorrowful Regret

BOUGAINVILLA

Passion

Bougainvillea spectabilis

Sydney Parkinson

Brazil. 1768

Passion

BUTTERCUP

Ingratitude & Childishness

Caltha palustris

F. Edward Hulme

London. Cassell & co.

Childishness

CAMELLIA

Longing & Persistent Desire

Camellia japonica

Marie Morren

Longing

_____

_____

_____

_____

_____

_____

_____

_____

_____

_____

_____

_____

_____

_____

_____

_____

_____

_____

_____

_____

_____

_____

_____

CANTURY BELL

Acknowledgement

Campanula medium

P. J. Redouté

Langlois sculp.

Acknowledgement

_____
_____
_____
_____
_____
_____
_____
_____
_____
_____
_____
_____
_____
_____
_____
_____
_____
_____
_____
_____
_____
_____
_____
_____
_____

CARNATION

I will never forget you

Dianthus caryophyllus

P.J.Redouté

Chapuy sculp.

I will never forget you

_____

_____

_____

_____

_____

_____

_____

_____

_____

_____

_____

_____

_____

_____

_____

_____

_____

_____

_____

_____

_____

_____

_____

CHAMOMILE

Energy in adversity

Anthemis nobilis

W. Clark

J. Stephenson & J. M. Churchill. 1836.

Energy in Adversity

CHERRY BLOSSOM

Impermanence & Transience

Prunus serrulata

Megata Morikaga

Library of Congress 1870

Impermanence

CHRYSANTHEMUM

Truth

Chrysanthemum

Truth

_____
_____
_____
_____
_____
_____
_____
_____
_____
_____
_____
_____
_____
_____
_____
_____
_____
_____
_____
_____
_____
_____
_____

HER HEART IS A WILDFLOWER

CHRYSANTHEMUM

R. Clift

Chrysanthemum

R. CLIFT

Her heart unfolds like a chrysanthemum, patiently, in its own time, in a way that can only be described as true. The unsteady soul of an artist, an eager pen in her hand, she is searching for something— someone— in this early morning mist.

Trees beginning to bud, seeds pushing their way through soil, butterflies waking with newfound wings— though she may be caught in a veil of fog, she can feel the earth coming alive again.

Another step forward– she sees the beauty in strange faces passing by. As her eyes change like colors in the evening sky, they hold a unique ability to see magnificence where others don't bother to look at all.

Another step, her soul beams and shines like stars in the night sky. The fog begins to clear and a smile curls across her petal-soft lips. She listens closely to the whispers of the stars and finally begins to believe that what they say is true— that maybe, just maybe, the woman she has been searching for has been here all along.

CLEMATIS

Mental beauty & Artifice

Clematis viticella

P. J. Redouté

Jarry sculp.

Mental Beauty

CLOVER

Luck & Promise

Trifolium

Luck

_____

_____

_____

_____

_____

_____

_____

_____

_____

_____

_____

_____

_____

_____

_____

_____

_____

_____

_____

_____

_____

_____

_____

CORNFLOWER

Hope in love & Patience

Centaurea cyanus

P. J. Redouté

Langlois sculp.

Patience

COSMOS

Harmony & Order

Cosmos bipinnatus

Miss Drake

J. Ridgeway 1837

Harmony

CROCUS

Youthful Gladness & Mirth

Crocus vernus

P. J. Redouté   Langlois sculp.

Youthful Gladness

CYPRESS

Mourning & Death

Cupressus

Mourning

DAFFODIL

Unrequited Love

Narcissus

P. J. Redouté

Bessin sculp.

Unrequited Love

_____
_____
_____
_____
_____
_____
_____
_____
_____
_____
_____
_____
_____
_____
_____
_____
_____
_____
_____
_____
_____
_____
_____
_____

DAHLIA

Everlasting Commitment

Dahlia double

P. J. Redouté

Langlois sculp.

Everlasting Commitment

_____

_____

_____

_____

_____

_____

_____

_____

_____

_____

_____

_____

_____

_____

_____

_____

_____

_____

_____

_____

_____

_____

_____

DAISY

Simplicity

Bellis perennis

P. J. Redouté

Langlois sculp.

Simplicity

DANDELION

Divination & Wishes will be granted

Taraxacum officinale

P. J. Redouté   Langlois sculp.

Divination

_____

_____

_____

_____

_____

_____

_____

_____

_____

_____

_____

_____

_____

_____

_____

_____

_____

_____

_____

_____

_____

_____

_____

_____

DAYLILY

Coquetry & Flirtation

Hemerocallis fulva

Coquetry

DOGWOOD

Enduring Love

Cornus florida

R. P. Smith

Philadelphia 1847

Enduring Love

HER HEART IS A WILDFLOWER

DOGWOOD

R. Clift

Cornus florida

R. CLIFT

Her heart shivers like a dogwood winter. Sparkling ice on branches. His sweater to keep her warm. They met when the earth was still. The air cold. His arms, her safety. Him, a kind of home she never knew she needed.

Trees tower overhead like giants. She wonders how big their hearts must be. Never realizing her own could fill the sea. A heart so long spent timid. She had always been good at leaving. The brave constellations taught her courage. The phases of the moon made her believe in coming back.

She longs to show him more of her favorite mountainsides and ocean tides. She tastes of adventure and he should know better than to try and tame a wild thing. She was never made to settle. She was made to soar.

Skin covered in celestial incandescence, he takes her hand. "Where to, wild one?" He asks. She smiles, soul on fire, and runs wherever the compass points. Freedom on her heels, and him, soaring beside her.

EDELWEISS

Noble Courage

Leantopodium nivale

Marina Lebedeva

Lemaris sculp.

Noble Courage

EGLANTINE

I wound to heal

Rosa rubiginosa

P. J. Redouté

Langlois sculp.

I wound to heal

FORGET-ME-NOT

Memories of Love

Myosotis sylvatica

P. J. Redouté

Langlois sculp.

Memories of Love

_____

_____

_____

_____

_____

_____

_____

_____

_____

_____

_____

_____

_____

_____

_____

_____

_____

_____

_____

_____

_____

_____

_____

_____

FOXGLOVE

Mystery & Deception

Digitalis purpurea

P.J.Redouté   Langlois sculp.

Deception

_____
_____
_____
_____
_____
_____
_____
_____
_____
_____
_____
_____
_____
_____
_____
_____
_____
_____
_____
_____
_____
_____
_____
_____
_____

FREESIA

Faithfulness through the seasons

Freesia refracta

F.W. Klatt   Gartenflora 1882

Faithfulness through the seasons

HER HEART IS A WILDFLOWER

FREESIA

R. Clift   Freesia refracta

R. CLIFT

Her heart is covered in freesia. Mysterious
& searching. Midsummer falls like rain
and washes the woodland in warmth.

Standing strong as a mountain, she wan-
ders through the trees. Losing herself in
nature, she can breathe. She is accompanied
by wild deer and buzzing bees. She follows
after them as hours pass by and runs fast-
er to keep up with their wings. Playing and
chasing and flying.

She is lucky to have friends such as these.
Some people only see outside through a
window, but she knows nature as her own.
Leaves glowing in the sunlight, her emer-
ald eyes sparkle like stars.

She captures each moment as a memory to
hold close, surrounding herself in flowers
& old polaroids. Her heart beats. She breathes
deep and the forest holds her closer. Never
truly alone, the wind whispers her name.
She smiles, knowing the best is yet to come.

GARDENIA
Secret Love

Gardenia jasminoides

Pieter Joseph de Pannemaeker

J. Linden 1889

Secret Love

_____
_____
_____
_____
_____
_____
_____
_____
_____
_____
_____
_____
_____
_____
_____
_____
_____
_____
_____
_____
_____
_____
_____
_____
_____

GERANIUM

Lovers' Meeting

Pelargonium?

P. J. Redouté

Langlois sculp.

Lovers' Meeting

GERBERA DAISY

Innocence

Gerbera

Dio

Flowsculp.

Innocence

GLADIOLUS

You pierce my heart

Gladiolus laccatus

P.J. Redouté

Chapuy sculp.

You pierce my heart

GLOXINIA

Love at first sight

Gloxinia perennis

P.J.Redouté

Langlois sculp.

Love at first sight

HAZEL

Reconciliation

Corylus avellana

Reconciliation

HELIOTROPE

Devotion

Heliotropium corymbosum

Vincent Brooks

1895

Devotion

HIMALAYAN POPPY

Possibilities

Meconopsis betonicifolia

Possibilities

_____
_____
_____
_____
_____
_____
_____
_____
_____
_____
_____
_____
_____
_____
_____
_____
_____
_____
_____
_____
_____
_____
_____
_____
_____

HOLLY

Foresight

Ilex aquifolium

P.J.Redouté

Trade 1801

Foresight

HOLLYHOCK

Female Ambition & Fertility

Alcea rosea

T.Fisher Unwin

1886

Fertility

_____
_____
_____
_____
_____
_____
_____
_____
_____
_____
_____
_____
_____
_____
_____
_____
_____
_____
_____
_____
_____
_____
_____

HYACINTH

Please forgive me

Hyacinthus orientalis

P.J.Redouté

Chapuy sculp.

Please forgive me

HER HEART IS A WILDFLOWER

HYACINTH

R. Clift   *Hyacinthus orientalis*

R. CLIFT

Her heart bundles up in hyacinth. Glowing
embers in the fireplace. A beloved paper-
back book in her lap. Wrinkles in the spine.
Sun stained & torn pages. She breathes in
new beginnings.

Exhales thoughts of him. Letting each
memory go one by one. She pulls her blan-
ket tight around her chest. A heart still
fragile to the touch. Grace & time. Grace &
time. Breathe in. Out. Grace & time.

She blinks the night from her her evergreen
eyes. Soothing words of her mother engulf
her mind. Strings musing on an acoustic
guitar. She can feel the music on her finger-
tips. Miles to go on the soles of her feet. Ink
bleeding from her veins for the thousands
to read. All she ever wishes to be is in her
reach. Eyes blink.

Early morning mist. Dawn rising. Gleam-
ing from tops of mountains to her kitchen
countertops. Jars of collected moments illu-
minated on the windowsill.

A warmth rushes through her as the floor-
boards creak. Her family wakes. Her favor-
ite recipe. Faded from use. Flame ignited.
Pages turn. Laughter in the air. Sweet scent
of morning. A peaceful moment collected.
A new day.

HYDRANGEA

Heartlessness

Hydrangea

P. J. Redouté

Langlois sculp.

Heartlessness

IRIS

Messages & Wisdom

Iris germanica

P. J. Redouté

Victor sculp.

Messages

IVY

Attatchment

Hedera helix

P. J. Redouté

M. Dufour sculp.

Attatchment

JASMINE

Sensuality

Jasminum officinale

P. J. Redouté   Moret sculp.

Sensuality

_____
_____
_____
_____
_____
_____
_____
_____
_____
_____
_____
_____
_____
_____
_____
_____
_____
_____
_____
_____
_____
_____
_____

LARKSPUR

Lightness & Levity

Delphinium

Levity

LAVENDER

Distrust

Lavandula angustifolia

W. Clark

1836

Distrust

LILAC

First emotions of love

Syringa

P.J.Redouté

Langlois sculp.

First emotions of love

LILY

Purity

Lilium candidum

P. J. Redouté

Victor sculp.

Purity

LILY OF THE VALLEY

Return of Happiness

Convallaria majalis

Return of Happiness

LOTUS

Enlightenment & Eloquence

Nelumbo nucifera

P.J.Redouté

Langlois sculp.

Enlightenment

LUPINE

Voraciousness & Imagination

Lupinus

John Lindley

J. Watts sculp.

Voraciousness

_____
_____
_____
_____
_____
_____
_____
_____
_____
_____
_____
_____
_____
_____
_____
_____
_____
_____
_____
_____
_____
_____
_____
_____
_____

MAGNOLIA

Dignity & Self-esteem

Magnolia grandiflora

P.J. Redouté

Traité 1801

Dignity

MARIGOLD

Grief

Tagetes

F. Edward Hulme   S. Hildert 1890

Grief

_____

_____

_____

_____

_____

_____

_____

_____

_____

_____

_____

_____

_____

_____

_____

_____

_____

_____

_____

_____

_____

_____

_____

_____

MOONFLOWER

Blossoming in dark times

Ipomoea alba

F.W. Horne

Flora Borinqueña

Blossoming in dark times

MOUNTAIN LAUREL

Ambition of a hero

Kalmia latifolia

P.J.Redouté

Traité 1801

Ambition of a hero

MYRTLE

Memory of Eden

Myrtus communis

Maria Sibylla Merian

1700

Memory of Eden

_____

_____

_____

_____

_____

_____

_____

_____

_____

_____

_____

_____

_____

_____

_____

_____

_____

_____

_____

_____

_____

_____

_____

NASTURTIUM

Victory & Triumph

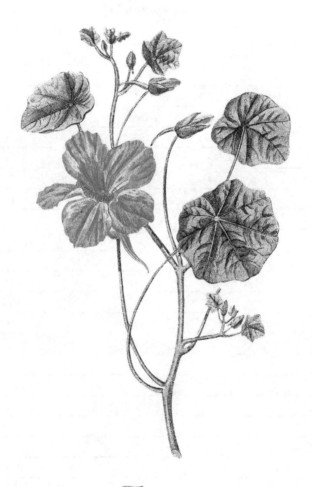

Tropaeolum

Victory

ORANGE BLOSSOM

Eternal Love & Marriage

Citrus sinensis

P. J. Redouté

Traité 1801

Eternal Love

ORCHID

Refinement & Mature Charm

Orchidaceae phalaenopsis

Refinement

PANSY

Thoughts & Think of me

Viola tricolor

P. J. Redouté

Langlois sculp.

Think of me

PASSION FLOWER

Faith & Superstition {if reversed}

Passiflora caerulea

Miss Drake

J. Watts sculp.

Faith

PEACE LILY

Forever at Peace

Spathiphyllum

Berthe Hoola van Nooten

1880

Forever at Peace

PEONY

Bashfulness & Compassion

Paeonia officinalis

A.J.Wendel

Flora 1868

Bashfulness

HER HEART IS A WILDFLOWER

PEONY

R. Clift　　　　　　　　　　　　*Paeonia officinalis*

R. CLIFT

Her heart an exquisite peony twirling in
the wind. Love spills from her outstretched
hands. Compassion covers the earth around
her like a blanket of snow.

The colors of dawn paint the ice in soft pas-
tel. A kind of magic is found here, witnessed
by her heartsome hazel eyes, that was once
thought to only ever exist in fairytales.

She follows the beating of her heart like a
trusted trail through icicle branches-- lead-
ing her to warmth. Winter has settled in.
Quiet & shy. She feels a sense of belonging
amongst the peace. The stillness. The prom-
ise of what will come.

She ties ribbons around her ankles and danc-
es through the snow-- effortless as a swan
in flight. An antique music box brought to
life.

Snowflakes fall and sparkle in the sky.
They melt on her palms reaching out. As
she moves to the melody she begins to realize
that the love she has been searching for can
never truly be found in any far off castle or
distance realm--but within her own spirit.

PERIWINKLE

Tender Recollections

Vinca minor

P. J. Redouté

Traité 1801

Tender Recollections

_____
_____
_____
_____
_____
_____
_____
_____
_____
_____
_____
_____
_____
_____
_____
_____
_____
_____
_____
_____
_____
_____
_____
_____
_____
_____
_____

PETUNIA

Anger & Resentment

Petunia

Anger

PHLOX

Our souls are united

Phlox

P. J. Redouté

Victor sculp.

Our souls are united

PLUMERIA

Intuition

Plumeria rubra

Intuition

_____

_____

_____

_____

_____

_____

_____

_____

_____

_____

_____

_____

_____

_____

_____

_____

_____

_____

_____

_____

_____

_____

_____

_____

POPPY

Sacrifice & Eternal Sleep

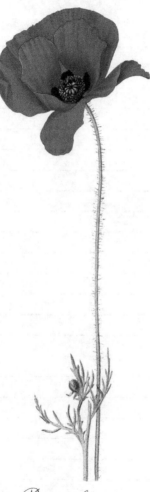

Papaver rhoeas

Sacrifice

PRIMROSE

I can't live without you

Primula vulgaris

P. J. Redouté

Bessin sculp.

I can't live without you

HER HEART IS A WILDFLOWER

PRIMROSE

R. Clift

Primula vulgaris

R. CLIFT

Her heart is as brave as primrose blooming alongside the first flowers of spring, before anything else has the courage to do so. Sunlight and golden fireflies trapped in her forest green eyes.

She relentlessly searches for the truth in deep waters, ever trusting the sea to keep her safe from harm. With love as constant as the waves kiss the shore, she kisses her children goodnight and wakes to see them another day older. Another day lived & loved.

As she grows into her authentic self, so do they. She gives away every tender piece of her heart, willingly, and although some may find this weary, it gives her strength. To care for those she loves is the greatest joy of her life, and because of that selflessness- she shines.

Even the stars lean in closer to catch a glimpse of her. Radiant & incandescent. She says hello with a love everlasting and goodbye with a light in her eyes that makes you believe in impossible things. The morning sun rises over the horizon to bring warmth to all it meets, and so does she.

As she walks among blooming trees, a cardinal sings its timeless song, and she can feel the hope within it. In this moment, she does not know fear.

RANUNCULUS

You are radiant with charms

Ranunculus asiaticus

Arentine H. Arendsen

G. Severeyns Brussel

You are radiant with charms

ROSE {RED}

Love & Romance

Rosa indica cruneta

Love

ROSE {PINK}

Please believe me

Rosa centifolia bullata

Please believe me

ROSE {WHITE}

I am worthy of you

Rosa campanulata alba

P.J.Redouté

Les Roses 1817

I am worthy of you

ROSE {YELLOW}

Jealousy & Decrease of love

Rosa sulfurea

Jealousy

_____
_____
_____
_____
_____
_____
_____
_____
_____
_____
_____
_____
_____
_____
_____
_____
_____
_____
_____
_____
_____
_____
_____

ROSEMARY

Remembrance

Rosmarinus officinalis

W. Clark

1826

Remembrance

_____
_____
_____
_____
_____
_____
_____
_____
_____
_____
_____
_____
_____
_____
_____
_____
_____
_____
_____
_____
_____
_____
_____
_____

RUDBECKIA

Justice

Rudbeckia hirta

F. Edward Hulme

S. Hilliard 1890

Justice

SAGE

Health & Long life

Salvia officinalis

P.J.Redouté

Traité 1801

Long life

SNAPDRAGON

Presumption & "No."

Antirrhinum

Presumption

_____
_____
_____
_____
_____
_____
_____
_____
_____
_____
_____
_____
_____
_____
_____
_____
_____
_____
_____
_____
_____
_____
_____
_____
_____

SNOWDROP

New Beginnings & Hope

Galanthus nivalis

P. J. Redouté

Liliaceæ 1805

New Beginnings

HER HEART IS A WILDFLOWER

SNOWDROP

R. Croft   Galanthus nivalis

R. CLIFT

Her heart blooms like a snowdrop in the
last days of winter. A new warmth of love
is making a home in her chest. She hopes
this one is here to stay.

Restless & unsettled. She craves freedom in
every sense of the word. Her mind wonders
from mountaintops to city sidewalks to
crashing tides all in the matter of moments.

She is a compass that cannot decide where to
point. An hourglass always running out of
sand. A thousand year old soul wrapped up
in the thought of tomorrow.

She loses herself in sunsets and finds her-
self there all the same. New life emerges as
snow melts into spring. A breath of hope. A
promise in rosebuds. A welcome heaviness
in her chest that assures her she is on the
right path.

Moving forward, every step fulfilled, ev-
ery minute cherished— she looks back at the
miles she has walked and smiles— for she
has come so far. For she still has so far to go,
so many hearts left to love, so much life left
to live— and in the end, she will have made
herself proud.

STARGAZER LILY

Evolution & Transcendence

Lilium orientalis

W.H.Fitch

1855

Transcendence

SUNFLOWER

Adoration & False Riches

Helianthus

Johan Teyler

1845

False Riches

SWEET PEA

Blissful Pleasure & Departure

Lathyrus odoratus

W. Clark

1826

Departure

SWEET WILLIAM

Gallantry & Chivalry

Dianthus barbatus

Gallantry

THISTLE

Misanthropy & Cynicism

Carduus

Mary Vaux Walcott

1888

Misanthropy

TIGER LILY

Pride & Riches

Lilium lancifolium

Pride

TRUMPET CREEPER

Separation

Campsis radicans

P.J.Redouté

Langlois sculp.

Separation

_____

_____

_____

_____

_____

_____

_____

_____

_____

_____

_____

_____

_____

_____

_____

_____

_____

_____

_____

_____

_____

_____

_____

TUBEROSE

Dangerous Pleasure

Polianthes tuberosa

P.J.Redouté

Langlois sculp.

Dangerous Pleasure

TULIP

Declaration of Love

Tulipa

P.J.Redouté

Langlois sculp.

Declaration of Love

_____

_____

_____

_____

_____

_____

_____

_____

_____

_____

_____

_____

_____

_____

_____

_____

_____

_____

_____

_____

_____

_____

_____

_____

_____

HER HEART IS A WILDFLOWER

TULIP

R. Clift   Cornus florida

R. CLIFT

Her heart blooms like brilliant tulips
reaching toward the midday sun. Her
warmth constant & everlasting. Her crys-
tal blue eyes carry assurance in their depth.

His dark eyes look to hers as lovers in the
moonlight gaze at the wonder of the heav-
ens. Mystified & entranced. To love a soul as
fierce as hers is no easy feat, but he does not
give up.

He adores her in every way a woman can
be adored and longs to show her what lies
beyond the horizon, a thousand cities and
endless seas. The oceans wait eagerly to be
touched by her as they listen to the sound of
his name coming from her lips— the only
music this universe can truly feel.

He circles the earth & captures the northern
lights themselves, bringing them home to
her- so she can catch a glimpse of eternity
and understand how rare the love they share
truly is.

As she holds celestial colors in her hands, he
whispers her name, and speaks his truth—
"As life goes on, through beauty and trage-
dy- I will cherish every inch of you, I will
be there to hold you close, and I will love
you—ardently— until the stars go cold."

VENICE MALLOW

Delicate & Fleeting Beauty

Hibiscus trionum

P.J.Redouté

Langlois sculp.

Fleeting Beauty

VIOLET

Modesty

Viola odorata

Mary Vaux Walcott

1886

Modesty

WALLFLOWER

Fidelity in Adversity

Cheiranthus cheiri

P.J.Redouté

Chapuy sculp.

Fidelity in Adversity

WEEPING WILLOW

Melancholy

Salix babylonica

P.J.Redouté

Traité 1801

Melancholy

WISTERIA

Welcome, fair stranger

Wisteria frutescens

Megata Morikaga

1870

Welcome, fair stranger

ZINNIA

I mourn your absence & Lasting love

Zinnia

G. Severeyns

Belgique horticole 1861

I mourn your absence

_____

_____

_____

_____

_____

_____

_____

_____

_____

_____

_____

_____

_____

_____

_____

_____

_____

_____

_____

_____

_____

_____

_____

_____

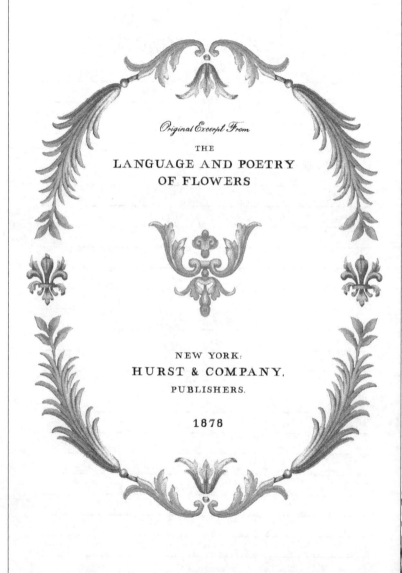

Original Excerpt From

THE

LANGUAGE AND POETRY
OF FLOWERS

NEW YORK:

HURST & COMPANY,

PUBLISHERS.

1878

Victorian Flower Dictionary

THE VOCABULARY.

PART THE FIRST.

———————

Abatina	*Fickleness.*
Abecedary	*Volatility.*
Acacia	*Friendship.*
Acacia, Rose or White	*Elegance.*
Acacia, Yellow	*Secret love.*
Acanthus	*The fine arts. Artifice.*
Acalia	*Temperance.*
Achillea Millefolia	*War.*
Aconite (Wolfsbane)	*Misanthropy.*
Aconite, Crowfoot	*Luster.*
Adonis, Flos	*Sad memories.*
African Marigold	*Vulgar minds.*
Agnus Castus	*Coldness. Indifference.*
Agrimony	*Thankfulness. Gratitude.*
Almond, Common	*Stupidity. Indiscretion.*
Almond, Flowering	*Hope.*
Almond, Laurel	*Perfidy*
Allspice	*Compassion.*
Aloe	*Grief. Superstition. Bitterness.*
Althaea Frutex (Syrian Mallow)	*Persuasion.*
Alyssum, Sweet	*Worth beyond beauty.*
Amaranth, Globe	*Immortality. Unfading love.*
Amaranth (Cockscomb)	*Foppery. Affectation.*
Amaryllis	*Pride. Determination. Worth*
Ambrosia	*Love returned. [beyond beauty.*
American Cowslip	*Divine beauty.*
American Elm	*Patriotism.*
American Linden	*Matrimony.*
American Starwort	*Welcome to a stranger. Cheer-*
Amethyst	*Admiration. [ful old age.*

Andromeda. . . . . *Self-sacrifice.*

Anemone (Zephyr Flower) . . . . *Sickness. Expectation.*

Anemone, Garden. . . . . *Forsaken.*

Angelica . . . . *Inspiration, or Magic.*

Angrec . . . . *Royalty.*

Apple . . . . *Temptation.* [*nation.*

Apple-blossom. . . . . *Preference. Knowledge & Illumi-*

Apple, Thorn . . . . *Deceitful charms.*

Apricot-blossom. . . . . *Doubt.* [*me.*

Arbor-vitæ. . . . . *Unchanging Friendship. Live for*

Arbutus. . . . . *Thee only do I love.*

Arum (Wake Robin) . . . . *Ardor. Zeal.*

Ash-leaved Trumpet Flower. . . . . *Separation.* [*safe.*

Ash, Mountain . . . . *Prudence, or With me you are*

Ash-tree. . . . . *Grandeur.*

Aspen-tree. . . . . *Lamentation, or fear.*

Aster, China. *Variety. Afterthought.*

Asphodel . . . . *My regrets follow you to the*

Auricula . . . . *Painting.* [*grave.*

Auricula, Scarlet . . . . *Avarice.*

Auricula, Yellow. . . . . *Splendor.*

Autumnal Leaves . . . . *Melancholy.* [*for me.*

Azalea . . . . *Temperance. Take care of yourself*

Bachelor's-button . . . . *Celibacy.*

Balm . . . . *Sympathy.*

Balm, Gentle . . . . *Pleasantry.*

Balm of Gilead . . . . *Cure. Relief.*

Balsam, Red . . . . *Touch me not. Impatient re-*

Balsam, Yellow . . . . *Impatience.* [*solves.*

Barberry . . . . *Sharpness of temper.*

Basil. . . . . *Hatred.*

Bay-leaf . . . . *I change but in death.*

Bay (Rose) Rhododendron . . . . *Danger. Beware.*

Bay-tree . . . . *Glory.*

Bay-wreath. . . . . *Reward of merit.*

Bearded Crepis . . . . *Protection.*

Beech-tree . . . . *Prosperity.*

Bee-orchis . . . . *Industry.*
Bee-ophrys. . . . . *Error.*
Begonia. . . . . *Uniqueness.*
Belladonna . . . . *Silence. Hush!*
Bellflower, Pyramidal. . . . . *Constancy.*
Bellflower. . . . . *Gratitude.*
Belvedere . . . . *I declare against you.*
Betony . . . . *Surprise.*
Bilberry. . . . . *Treachery.*
Bindweed, Great . . . . *Insinuation. Importunity.*
Bindweed, Small. . . . . *Humility.*
Birch . . . . *Meekness.*
Birdsfoot (Trefoil) . . . . *Revenge.*
Bittersweet (Nightshade). . . . . *Truth.*
Black Poplar . . . . *Courage. Affliction.*
Blackthorn . . . . *Difficulty.*
Bladder-nut Tree . . . . *Frivolity. Amusement.*
Bluebottle (Centaury) . . . . *Delicacy.*
Bluebell. . . . . *Constancy. Sorrowful regret.*
Blue-flower Greek Valerian . . . . *Rupture.*
Bonus Henricus . . . . *Goodness.*
Borage . . . . *Bluntness.*
Box-tree . . . . *Stoicism.*
Bramble. . . . . *Lowliness. Envy. Remorse.*
Branch of Currants . . . . *You please all.*
Branch of Thorns. . . . . *Severity. Rigor.*
Bridal Rose. . . . . *Happy love.*
Broom. . . . . *Humility. Neatness.*
Browallia Jamisonii . . . . *Could you bear poverty?*
Buckbean. . . . . *Calm repose.*
Bud of White Rose . . . . *A heart ignorant of love.*
Bugloss . . . . *Falsehood.*
Bulrush . . . . *Indiscretion. Docility.*
Bundle of Reeds, with their Panicles . . . . *Music.*
Burr. . . . . *Rudeness. You weary me.*
Burdock. . . . . *Importunity. Touch me not.*
Buttercup (Kingcup) . . . . *Ingratitude. Childishness.*
Butterfly-orchis . . . . *Gayety.*

Butterfly-weed . . . . *Let me go.*

Cabbage . . . . *Profit.*
Cacalia . . . . *Adulation.*
Cactus . . . . *Warmth.*
Calla Æthiopica . . . . *Magnificent Beauty.*
Calycanthus . . . . *Benevolence.*
Camellia Japonica, Red . . . . *Longing. Persistent Desire.*
Camellia, White . . . . *Perfected loveliness.*
Campanula Pyramida . . . . *Aspiring.*
Camphire . . . . *Fragrance.*
Canary-grass . . . . *Perseverance.*
Candytuft . . . . *Indifference.*
Canterbury-bell . . . . *Acknowledgement.*
Cape Jasmine . . . . *I am too happy.*
Cardamine . . . . *Paternal error.*
Carnation, Deep Red . . . . *Alas! for my poor heart.*
Carnation, Pink . . . . *I will never forget you.*
Carnation, Striped . . . . *Refusal.*
Carnation, Yellow . . . . *Disdain.*
Cardinal-flower . . . . *Distinction.*
Catchfly . . . . *Snare.*
Catchfly, Red . . . . *Youthful love.*
Catchfly, White . . . . *Betrayed.*
Cattleya . . . . *Mature charms. Matronly grace.*
Cedar . . . . *Strength.*
Cedar of Lebanon . . . . *Incorruptible.*
Cedar-leaf . . . . *I live for thee.*
Celandine, Lesser . . . . *Joys to come.*
Cereus, Creeping . . . . *Modest genius.*
Centaury . . . . *Delicacy.*
Chamomile . . . . *Energy in adversity.*
Champignon . . . . *Suspicion.*
Checkered Fritillary . . . . *Persecution.*
Cherry-tree, White . . . . *Good education.*
Cherry-blossom . . . . *Impermanence.*
Chesnut Tree . . . . *Do me justice.*
Chinese Primrose . . . . *Lasting Love.*

Chickweed . . . . *Rendezvous.*
Chicory . . . . *Frugality.*
China-aster . . . . *Variety.*
China-aster, Double . . . . *I partake of your sentiments.*
China-aster, Single . . . . *I will think of it.*
China or Indian Pink. . . . . *Aversion.*
China-rose . . . . *Beauty always new.*
Chinese Chrysanthemum. . . . . *Cheerfulness under adversity.*
Chorozema Varium . . . . *You have many lovers.*
Christmas-rose . . . . *Relieve my anxiety.*
Chrysanthemum, Red . . . . *I love.*
Chrysanthemum, White . . . . *Truth.*
Chrysanthemum, Yellow . . . . *Slighted love.*
Cineraria . . . . *Always delightful.*
Cinquefoil . . . . *Maternal affection.*
Circæa . . . . *Spell.*
Cistus, or Rock-rose . . . . *Popular favour.*
Cistus, Gum . . . . *I shall die to-morrow.*
Citron. . . . . *Ill-natured beauty. [delights me.*
Clarkia . . . . *The ariety of your conversation*
Clematis . . . . *Mental beauty. Artifice.*
Clematis, Evergreen . . . . *Poverty.*
Clianthus . . . . *Worldliness. Self-seeking*
Clotbur . . . . *Rudeness. Pertinacity.*
Cloves. . . . . *Dignity.*
Clover, Four-leaved. . . . . *Be mine.*
Clover, Red . . . . *Industry.*
Clover, White . . . . *Think of me. Promise.*
Cobæa . . . . *Gossip.*
Cockscomb (Amaranth) . . . . *Foppery. Affectation. Singulari-*
Colchicum, or Meadow-saffron . . . . *My best days are past.* [ty.
Coltsfoot . . . . *Justice shall be done.*
Columbine . . . . *Folly.*
Columbine, Purple . . . . *Resolved to win.*
Columbine, Red. . . . . *Anxious and trembling.*
Convolvulus . . . . *Bonds.*
Convolvulus Blue, Minor. . . . . *Repose. Night.*
Convolvulus Major . . . . *Extinguished hopes.* [affecction.

Convolvulus, Pink . . . . *Worth, and judicious and tender*
Corchorus . . . . *Impatient of absence.*
Coreopsis . . . . *Always cheerful.*
Coreopsis Arkansa . . . . *Love at first sight.*
Coriander . . . . *Hidden worth.*
Corn . . . . *Riches.*
Corn, Broken . . . . *Quarrel.*
Cornbottle . . . . *Delicacy.*
Corncockle . . . . *Gentility.*
Corn-straw . . . . *Agreement.*
Cornel-tree . . . . *Duration.*
Coronella . . . . *Success crown your wishes.*
Cosmelia Subra . . . . *The charm of a blush.*
Cowslip . . . . *Pensiveness. Grace.*
Cowslip (American) . . . . *Divine beauty.*
Crab-blossom . . . . *Ill-nature.*
Cranberry . . . . *Cure for heartache.*
Creeping Cereus . . . . *Horror.*
Cress . . . . *Stability. Power.*
Crocus . . . . *Abuse not. Impatience.*
Crocus, Spring . . . . *Youthful gladness.*
Crocus (Saffron) . . . . *Mirth. Cheerfulness.*
Crown Imperial . . . . *Majesty. Power.*
Crowsbill . . . . *Envy.*
Crowfoot . . . . *Ingratitude.*
Crowfoot (Aconite-leaved) . . . . *Luster.*
Cuckoo-plant . . . . *Ardor.*
Cudweed, American . . . . *Unceasing remembrance.*
Currant . . . . *Thy frown will kill me.*
Cuscuta . . . . *Meanness.*
Cyclamen . . . . *Diffidence.*
Cypress . . . . *Death. Mourning.*

Daffodil . . . . *Regard. Unrequited love.*
Dahlia . . . . *Everlasting Commitment.*
Daisy . . . . *Innocence and Hope. Simplicity.*
Daisy, Garden . . . . *I share your sentiments.*
Daisy, Michaelmas . . . . *Farewell, or Afterthought.*

Daisy, Parti-coloured . . . . *Beauty.*
Daisy, Wild . . . . *I will think of it.*
Damask-rose . . . . *Brilliant complexion.*
Dandelion . . . . *Rustic oracle. Divination.*
Daphne . . . . *Glory. Immortality.*
Daphne-odora . . . . *Painting the lily.*
Darnel . . . . *Vice*
Dead Leaves . . . . *Sadness.*
Dewplant . . . . *A serenade.*
Dianthus . . . . *Make haste.*
Diosma . . . . *Your simple elegance charms me.*
Dipteracanthus Spectabilis. . . . . *Fortitude.*
Diplademia Crassinoda . . . . *You are too bold.*
Dittany of Crete . . . . *Birth.*
Dittany of Crete, White . . . . *Passion.*
Dock . . . . *Patience.*
Dodder of Thyme. . . . . *Baseness.*
Dogsbane . . . . *Deceit. Falsehood.*
Dogwood . . . . *Durability.*
Dragon-plant. *Snare.*
Dragonwort. . . . . *Horror.*
Dried Flax . . . . *Utility.*

Ebony Tree . . . . *Blackness.*
Echites Atropurpurea. . . . . *Be warned in time.*
Eglantine (Sweetbrier) . . . . *Poetry. I wound to heal.*
Elder . . . . *Zealousness.*
Elm . . . . *Dignity.*
Enchanter's Nightshade . . . . *Witchcraft. Sorcery.*
Endive . . . . *Frugality.*
Eschscholtzia . . . . *Do not refuse me.*
Eupatorium. . . . . *Delay.*
Evening Primrose . . . . *Silent love.*
Ever-bowing Candytuft. . . . . *Indifference.*
Evergreen Clematis. . . . . *Poverty.*
Evergreen Thorn . . . . *Solace in adversity.*
Everlasting . . . . *Never-ceasing remembrance.*
Everlasting Pea . . . . *Lasting pleasure.*

Fennel. . . . . *Worthy all praise. Strength.*
Fern. . . . . *Fascination. Magic. Sincerity.*
Ficoides (Iceplant) . . . . *Your looks freeze me.*
Fig. . . . . *Argument.*
Fig-marigold. . . . . *Idleness.*
Fig-tree. . . . . *Prolific.*
Filbert . . . . *Reconciliation.*
Fir. . . . . *Time.*
Fir-tree. . . . . *Elevation.*
Flax . . . . *Domestic Industry. Fate. I feel*
Flax-leaved Golden-locks . . . . *Tardiness.* [*your kindness.*
Fleur-de-lis . . . . *Flame. I burn.*
Fleur-de-luce . . . . *Fire.*
Flowering Fern . . . . *Reverie.*
Flowering Reed . . . . *Confidence in Heaven.*
Flower-of-an-Hour . . . . *Delicate Beauty.*
Fly-orchis . . . . *Error.*
Flytrap . . . . *Deceit.*
Fool's Parsley . . . . *Silliness.*
Forget-Me-Not . . . . *Forget me not. Memory of love.*
Foxglove . . . . *Insincerity. Mystery. Deception.*
Foxtail-grass . . . . *Sporting.*
Franciscea Latifolia. . . . . *Beware of false friends.*
French Honeysuckle . . . . *Rustic beauty.*
French Marigold . . . . *Jealousy.*
French Willow. *Bravery and Humanity.*
Frog-ophrys . . . . *Disgust.*
Fuller's Teasel. *Misanthropy.*
Fumitory . . . . *Spleen.*
Fuchsia, Scarlet . . . . *Taste.*
Furze, or Gorse . . . . *Love for all seasons. Anger.*

Garden Anemone . . . . *Forsaken.*
Garden Chervil . . . . *Sincerity.*
Garden Daisy . . . . *I partake of your sentiments.*
Garden Marigold . . . . *Uneasiness.*
Garden Ranunculus. . . . . *You are rich in attractions.*
Garden Sage . . . . *Esteem.*

Gardenia . . . . *Refinement. Secret love.*
Garland of Roses . . . . *Reward of virtue.*
Gentian. . . . . *I love you best when you are sad.*
Germander Speedwell . . . . *Facility.*
Geranium . . . . *Lovers' meeting.*
Geranium, Dark. . . . . *Melancholy.*
Geranium, Horseshoe-leaf. . . . . *Stupidity.*
Geranium, Ivy. *Bridal favour.*
Geranium, Lemon . . . . *Unexpected meeting.*
Geranium, Nutmeg . . . . *Expected meeting.*
Geranium, Oak-leaved . . . . *True friendship.*
Geranium, Penciled. . . . . *Ingenuity.*
Geranium, Rose-scented. . . . . *Preference.*
Geranium, Scarlet . . . . *Comforting.*
Geranium, Silver-leaved . . . . *Recall.*
Geranium, Wild. . . . . *Steadfast piety.*
Gillyflower. . . . . *Bonds of affection.* [*heart.*
Gladioli. . . . . *Ready armed. You pierce my*
Glory-flower . . . . *Glorious beauty.*
Goat's-rue . . . . *Reason.*
Golden-rod. . . . . *Precaution.*
Gooseberry. . . . . *Anticipation.*
Gourd. . . . . *Extent. Bulk.*
Grammanthus Chloraflora . . . . *Your temper is too hasty.*
Grape, Wild . . . . *Charity.*
Grass . . . . *Submission. Utility.*
Guelder-rose. . . . . *Winter. Age.*

Handflower-tree. . . . . *Warning.*
Harebell . . . . *Submission. Grief.*
Hawkweed . . . . *Quick-sightedness.*
Hawthorn. . . . . *Hope.*
Hazel . . . . *Reconciliation.*
Heartsease, or Pansy . . . . *Thoughts*
Heath . . . . *Solitude.*
Helenium. . . . . *Tears.*
Heliotrope . . . . *Devotion; or, I turn to thee.*
Hellebore. . . . . *Scandal. Calumny.*

Helmet-flower (Monkshood). . . . . *Knight-errantry.*
Hemlock . . . . *You will be my death.*
Hemp . . . . *Fate.*
Henbane . . . . *Imperfection.*
Hepatica . . . . *Confidence.*
Hibiscus . . . . *Delicate beauty.*
Holly . . . . *Foresight.*
Holly Herb. . . . . *Enchantment.*
Hollyhock . . . . *Female ambition. Fertility.*
Honesty. . . . . *Honesty. Fascination.*
Honeyflower . . . . *Love sweet and secret.*
Honeysuckle . . . . *Generous and devoted affection.*
Honeysuckle, Coral . . . . *The color of my fate.*
Honeysuckle, French . . . . *Rustic beauty.*
Hop . . . . *Injustice.*
Hornbeam . . . . *Ornament.*
Horse-chesnut . . . . *Luxury.*
Hortensia. . . . . *You are cold.*
Houseleek. . . . . *Vivacity. Domestic industry.*
Houstonia. . . . . *Content.*
Hoya . . . . *Sculpture.*
Humble-plant . . . . *Despondency.*
Hundred-leaved Rose. . . . . *Dignity of mind.*
Hyacinth . . . . *Sport. Game. Play.*
Hyacinth, Purple . . . . *Sorrowful. Please forgive me.*
Hyacinth, White . . . . *Unobtrusive loveliness.*
Hydrangea . . . . *A boaster. Heartlessness.*
Hyssop . . . . *Cleanliness.*

Iceland-moss. *Health.*
Iceplant. . . . . *Your looks freeze me.*
Imbricata. . . . . *Sentiments of honor.*
Imperial-montague . . . . *Power.*
Indian-cress . . . . *Warlike trophy.*
Indian-jasmine (Ipomœa) . . . . *Attachment.*
Indian-pink (double) . . . . *Always lovely.*
Indian-plum . . . . *Privation.*
Iris . . . . *Messages.*

Iris, German. *Flame.*
Ivy. . . . . *Attatchment. Fidelity. Marriage.*
Ivy, Sprig of, with Tendrils . . . . *Assiduous to please.*

Jacob's Ladder . . . . *Come down.*
Japan-rose . . . . *Beauty is your only attraction.*
Japanese Lilies. . . . . *You can not decieve me.*
Jasmine . . . . *Amiability.*
Jasmine, Cape . . . . *Transport of joy.*
Jasmine, Carolina . . . . *Separation.*
Jasmine, Indian . . . . *I attach myself to you.*
Jasmine, Spanish . . . . *Sensuality.*
Jasmine, Yellow . . . . *Grace and elegance.*
Jonquil . . . . *I desire a return of affection.*
Judas-tree . . . . *Unbelief. Betrayal.*
Julienne, White . . . . *Despair not; God is everywhere.*
Juniper . . . . *Succour. Protection.   [ness.*
Justicia . . . . *The perfection of female loveli-*

Kennedia . . . . *Mental Beauty.*
Kingcups . . . . *Desire of Riches.*

Laburnum . . . . *Forsaken. Pensive Beauty.*
Lady's Slipper . . . . *Capricious Beauty. Win me and*
Lagerstræmia, Indian. . . . . *Eloquence.   [wear me.*
Lantana . . . . *Rigor.*
Lapageria Rosea. . . . . *There is no unalloyed good.*
Larch . . . . *Audacity. Boldness.*
Larkspur . . . . *Lightness. Levity.*
Larkspur, Pink. . . . . *Fickleness.*
Larkspur, Purple. . . . . *Haughtiness.*
Laurel. . . . . *Glory.*
Laurel, Common, (in flower) . . . . *Perfidy.*
Laurel, Ground . . . . *Perseverance.*
Laurel, Mountain . . . . *Ambition.*
Laurel-leaved Magnolia . . . . *Dignity.*
Laurestina . . . . *A token. I die if neglected.*
Lavender . . . . *Distrust.*

Leaves, Dead. . . . . *Melancholy.*
Lemon . . . . *Zest.*
Lemon-blossoms. . . . . *Fidelity in Love.*
Leschenaultia Splendens . . . . *You are charming.*
Lettuce . . . . *Cold-heartedness.*
Lichen . . . . *Dejection. Solitude.*
Lilac, Field. . . . . *Humility.*
Lilac, Purple. *First emotions of love.*
Lilac, White. . . . . *Joy of youth.*
Lily, Day. . . . . *Coquetry. Flirtation.*
Lily, Imperial . . . . *Majesty.*
Lily, White. . . . . *Purity. Sweetness.*
Lily, Yellow . . . . *Falsehood. Gaiety.*
Lily of the Valley. . . . . *Return of happiness.*
Linden or Lime Trees . . . . *Conjugal love.*
Lint . . . . *I feel my obligations.*
Live-oak . . . . *Liberty.*
Liverwort. . . . . *Confidence.*
Licorice, Wild. . . . . *I declare against you.*
Lobelia . . . . *Malevolence.*
Locust-tree. . . . . *Elegance.*
Locust-tree (green) . . . . *Affection beyond the grave.*
London Pride . . . . *Frivolity.*
Lote-tree. . . . . *Concord.*
Lotus . . . . *Eloquence. Repose. Enlighten-*
Lotus-flower . . . . *Estranged love.*   *[ment.*
Lotus-leaf . . . . *Recantation.*
Love-in-a-mist . . . . *Perplexity.*
Love-lies-bleeding . . . . *Hopeless, not heartless.*
Lucerne. . . . . *Life.*
Lupine . . . . *Voraciousness. Imagination.*

Madder . . . . *Calumny.*
Magnolia . . . . *Love of Nature. Dignity.*
Magnolia, Swamp. . . . . *Perseverance.*
Mallow . . . . *Mildness.*
Mallow, Marsh . . . . *Beneficence.*
Mallow, Syrian . . . . *Consumed by love.*

Mallow, Venetian . . . . *Delicate, fleeting beauty.*
Malon Creeana . . . . *Will you share my fortunes?*
Manchineal-tree. . . . . *Falsehood.*
Mandrake. *Horror.*
Maple. . . . . *Reserve.*
Marianthus. . . . . *Hope for better days.*
Marigold . . . . *Grief.*
Marigold, African. . . . . *Vulgar minds.*
Marigold, French . . . . *Jealousy.*
Marigold, Prophetic. . . . . *Prediction.*
Marigold and Cypress . . . . *Despair.*
Marjoram. *Blushes.*
Marvel of Peru . . . . *Timidity.*
Meadow-lychnis. . . . . *Wit.*
Meadow-saffron . . . . *My best days are past.*
Meadowsweet . . . . *Uselessness.*
Mercury . . . . *Goodness.*
Mesembryanthemum . . . . *Idleness.*
Mezereon. *Desire to please.*
Michaelmas-daisy. . . . . *Afterthought.*
Mignionette . . . . *Your qualities surpass your*
Milfoil . . . . *War.*   [*charms.*
Milkvetch. *Your presence softens my pains.*
Milkwort . . . . *Hermitage.*
Mimosa (Sensitive-plant) . . . . *Sensitiveness.*
Mint. . . . . *Virtue.*
Mistletoe . . . . *I surmount difficulties. Kiss me.*
Mitraria Coccinea . . . . *Indolence. Dullness.*
Mock-orange. . . . . *Counterfeit.*
Monarda Amplexicaulis . . . . *Your whims are unbearable.*
Monkshood. . . . . *A deadly foe is near.*
Monkshood (Helmet-flower). . . . . *Chivalry. Knight-errantry.*
Moonwort . . . . *Forgetfulness.*
Morning-glory. . . . . *Affectation.*
Moschatel . . . . *Weakness.*
Moss . . . . *Maternal love.*
Mosses . . . . *Ennui.*
Mossy Saxifrage . . . . *Affection.*

Motherwort .... *Concealed love.*
Mountain Ash .... *Prudence.*
Mourning Bride .... *Unfortunate attachment. I have*
Mouse-eared Chickweed .... *Ingenuous simplicity.* [*lost all.*
Mouse-eared Scorpion-grass ...... *Forget me not.*
Moving-plant .... *Agitation.*
Mudwort .... *Happiness. Tranquillity.*
Mulberry-tree, Black .... *I shall not survive you.*
Mulberry-tree, White .... *Wisdom.* [*trust you.*
Mushroom .... *Suspicion; or, I can't entirely*
Musk-plant .... *Weakness.*
Mustard Seed .... *Indifference.*
Myrobalan .... *Privation.*
Myrrh .... *Gladness.*
Myrtle .... *Love. Memory of Eden.*

Narcissus .... *Egotism.*
Nasturtium .... *Patriotism. Triumph. Victory.*
Nemophila .... *Success everywhere.*
Nettle, Common Stinging .... *You are spiteful.*
Nettle, Burning .... *Slander.*
Nettle-tree .... *Conceit.*
Night-blooming Cereus .... *Transient beauty.*
Night Convolvulus .... *Night.*
Nightshade .... *Falsehood.*

Oak-leaves .... *Bravery.*
Oak-tree .... *Hospitality.*
Oak, White .... *Independence.*
Oats .... *The witching soul of music.*
Oleander .... *Beware.*
Olive .... *Peace.* [*your loveliness.*
Orange-blossoms .... *Marriage. Your purity equals*
Orange-flowers .... *Chastity. Bridal festivities.*
Orange-tree .... *Generosity.*
Orchis .... *A belle.*
Osier .... *Frankness.*
Osmunda .... *Dreams.*

Oxeye . . . . *Patience.*
Oxlip . . . . *Speak out.*

Palm . . . . *Victory.*
Pansy . . . . *Thoughts. Think of me.*
Parsley . . . . *Festivity. To win.*
Pasqueflower . . . . *You have no claims.*
Passionflower . . . . *Superstition (when reversed) or*
Patience Dock . . . . *Patience.   [Faith if erect.*
Pea, Everlasting . . . . *An appointed meeting. Lasting*
Pea, Sweet . . . . *Departure.   [Pleasure.*
Peach . . . . *Your charms are unequaled.*
Peach-blossom . . . . *I am your captive.*
Pear . . . . *Affection.*
Pear-tree . . . . *Comfort.*
Pennyroyal . . . . *Flee away.*
Peony . . . . *Shame. Bashfulness. Compassion.*
Peppermint . . . . *Warmth of feeling.   [lections.*
Periwinkle, Blue . . . . *Early friendship. Tender Recol-*
Periwinkle, White . . . . *Pleasures of memory.*
Persicaria . . . . *Restoration.*
Persimmon . . . . *Bury me amid Nature's beauties.*
Peruvian Heliotrope . . . . *Devotion.   [ger. Resentment.*
Petunia . . . . *Your presence soothes me; or An-*
Pheasant's-eye . . . . *Remembrance.*
Phlox . . . . *Unanimity. Our souls are united.*
Pigeon-berry . . . . *Indifference.*
Pimpernel . . . . *Change. Assignation.*
Pine . . . . *Pity.*
Pineapple . . . . *You are perfect.*
Pine, Pitch . . . . *Philosophy.*
Pine, Spruce . . . . *Hope in adversity.*
Pink . . . . *Boldness.*
Pink, Carnation . . . . *Woman's love.*
Pink, Indian Double . . . . *Always lovely.*
Pink, Indian Single . . . . *Aversion.*
Pink, Mountain . . . . *Aspiring.*
Pink, Red Double . . . . *Pure and ardent love.*

Pink, Single . . . . *Pure love.*
Pink, Variegated . . . . *Refusal.*
Pink, White . . . . *Ingeniousness. Talent.*
Plane-tree . . . . *Genius.*
Plum, Indian . . . . *Privation.*
Plum-tree . . . . *Fidelity.*
Plum, Wild . . . . *Independence.*
Polyanthus . . . . *Pride of riches.*
Polyanthus, Crimson . . . . *The heart's mystery.*
Polyanthus, Lilac . . . . *Confidence.*
Pomegranate . . . . *Foolishness.*
Pomegranate-flower . . . . *Nature. Elegance.*
Poor Robin . . . . *Compensation, or an equivalent.*
Poplar, Black . . . . *Courage.*
Poplar, White . . . . *Time.*   [*sleep.*
Poppy, Red . . . . *Consolation. Sacrifice. Eternal*
Poppy, Scarlet . . . . *Fantastic extravagance.*
Poppy, White . . . . *Sleep. My bane. My antidote.*
Potato . . . . *Benevolence.*
Potentilla . . . . *I claim at least your esteem.*
Prickly-pear . . . . *Satire.*
Pride of China . . . . *Dissension.*   [*live without you.*
Primrose . . . . *Early youth & sadness. I can't*
Primrose, Evening . . . . *Inconstancy.*
Primrose, Red . . . . *Unpatronized merit.*
Privet . . . . *Prohibition.*
Purple Clover . . . . *Provident.*
Pyrus Japonica . . . . *Fairies' fire.*

Quaking-grass . . . . *Agitation.*
Quamoclit . . . . *Busybody.*
Queen's Rocket . . . . *You are the queen of coquettes.*
Quince . . . . *Temptation.*   [*Fashion.*

Ragged-robin . . . . *Wit.*
Ranunculus . . . . *You are radiant with charms.*
Ranunculus, Garden . . . . *You are rich in attractions.*
Ranunculus, Wild . . . . *Ingratitude.*

Raspberry . . . . *Remorse.*
Ray-grass. . . . . *Vice.*
Red Catchfly. *Youthful love.*
Reed. . . . . *Complaisance. Music.*
Reed, Split . . . . *Indiscretion.*
Rhododendron (Rosebay). . . . . *Danger. Beware.*
Rhubarb . . . . *Advice.*
Rocket . . . . *Rivalry.*
Rose-mundi . . . . *Variety.*
Rose, Austrian. . . . . *Thou art all that is lovely.*
Rose, Bridal . . . . *Happy love.*
Rose, Burgundy . . . . *Unconscious beauty.*
Rose, Cabbage. . . . . *Ambassador of love.*
Rose, Campion . . . . *Only deserve my love.*
Rose, Caroline. . . . . *Love is dangerous.*
Rose, China . . . . *Beauty always new.*
Rose, Christmas. . . . . *Tranquillize my anxiety.*
Rose, Daily . . . . *Thy smile I aspire to.*
Rose, Damask . . . . *Brilliant complexion.*
Rose, Deep Red. . . . . *Bashful shame.*
Rose, Dog . . . . *Pleasure and pain.*
Rose, Guelder . . . . *Winter. Age.*
Rose, Hundred-leaved . . . . *Pride.*
Rose, Japan. . . . . *Beauty is your only attraction.*
Rose, Maiden-blush. . . . . *If you love me, you will find it*
Rose, Montiflora. . . . . *Grace.* [*out.*
Rose, Musk. . . . . *Capricious beauty.*
Rose, Musk, Cluster . . . . *Charming.*
Rose, Red . . . . *Love.*
Rose, Single . . . . *Simplicity.*
Rose, Thornless. . . . . *Early attachment.*
Rose, Unique . . . . *Call me not beautiful.*
Rose, White . . . . *I am worthy of you.*
Rose, White (withered) . . . . *Transient impressions.*
Rose, Yellow. *Decrease of love. Jealously.*
Rose, York and Lancaster . . . . *War.*
Rose, (full-blown, over two buds) . . . . *Secrecy.*
Rose, White and Red together . . . . *Unity.*

Roses, Crown of. . . . . *Reward of virtue.*
Rosebud, Red . . . . *Pure and lovely.*
Rosebud, White. . . . . *Girlhood.*
Rosebud, Moss. . . . . *Confession of love.*
Rose-leaf. . . . . *You may hope.*
Rosemary. . . . . *Remembrance.*
Rudbeckia . . . . *Justice.*
Rue . . . . *Disdain.*
Rush. . . . . *Docility.*
Rye-grass. . . . . *Changeable disposition.*

Saffron . . . . *Beware of excess.*
Saffron Crocus. *Mirth.*
Saffron, Meadow . . . . *My happiest days are past.*
Sage. . . . . *Domestic virtue.*
Sage, Garden . . . . *Esteem. Health. Long life.*
Sainfoin. . . . . *Agitation.*
Saint John's Wort . . . . *Animosity. Superstition.*
Salvia, Blue . . . . *Wisdom.*
Salvia, Red. . . . . *Energy.*
Saxifrage, Mossy . . . . *Affection.*
Scabious . . . . *Unfortunate love.*
Scabious, Sweet . . . . *Widowhood.*
Scarlet Lychnis . . . . *Sunbeaming eyes.*
Schinus . . . . *Religious enthusiasm.*
Scotch Fir . . . . *Elevation.*
Sensitive-plant. *Sensibility.*
Senvy . . . . *Indifference.*
Shamrock. . . . . *Light-heartedness.*
Shepherd's Purse . . . . *I offer you my all.*
Siphocampylos. *Resolved to be noticed.*
Snakesfoot . . . . *Horror.*
Snapdragon. . . . . *Presumption. Also, "No."*
Snowball . . . . *Bound.*
Snowdrop. . . . . *Hope. New beginnings.*
Sorrel . . . . *Affection.*
Sorrel, Wild . . . . *Wit ill-timed.*
Sorrel, Wood. . . . . *Joy.*

Southernwood . . . . *Jest. Bantering.*
Spanish Jasmine . . . . *Sensuality.*
Spearmint . . . . *Warmth of sentiment.*
Speedwell. . . . . *Female fidelity.*
Speedwell, Germander . . . . *Facility.*
Speedwell, Spiked . . . . *Semblance.*
Spider-ophrys . . . . *Adroitness.*
Spiderwort . . . . *Esteem, not love.*
Spiked Willow-herb. . . . . *Pretension.*
Spindle-tree . . . . *Your charms are engraven on my*
Star of Bethlehem. . . . . *Purity.* [*heart.*
Starwort . . . . *Afterthought.*
Starwort, American. . . . . *Cheerfulness in old age.*
Stock . . . . *Lasting beauty.*
Stock, Ten-week . . . . *Promptness.*
Stonecrop. . . . . *Tranquillity.*
Straw (broken). . . . . *Rupture of a contract.*
Straw (whole) . . . . *Union.*
Strawberry-blossoms . . . . *Foresight.*
Strawberry-tree . . . . *Esteem, not love.*
Sultan, Lilac. *I forgive you.*
Sultan, White . . . . *Sweetness.*
Sultan, Yellow . . . . *Contempt.*
Sumach, Venice . . . . *Splendor.*
Sunflower, Dwarf . . . . *Adoration.*
Sunflower, Tall . . . . *Haughtiness. False Riches.*
Swallow-wort . . . . *Cure for heartache.*
Sweet Basil. . . . . *Good wishes.*
Sweetbrier, American. . . . . *Simplicity.*
Sweetbrier, European. . . . . *I wound to heal.*
Sweetbrier, Yellow . . . . *Decrease of love.*
Sweet Pea . . . . *Blissful pleasures. Departure.*
Sweet Sultan. *Felicity.*
Sweet Sedge . . . . *Resignation.*
Sweet-william . . . . *Gallantry.*
Sycamore. . . . . *Curiosity.*
Syringa . . . . *Memory.*
Syringa, Carolina . . . . *Disappointment.*

Tamarisk . . . . *Crime.*
Tansy, Wild . . . . *I declare war against you.*
Teasel . . . . *Misanthropy.*
Tendrils of Climbing-plants . . . . *Ties.*
Thistle, Common . . . . *Austerity. Independence.*
Thistle, Fuller's . . . . *Misanthropy.*
Thistle, Scotch . . . . *Retaliation.*
Thornapple . . . . *Deceitful charms.*
Thorn, Branch of . . . . *Severity.*
Thrift . . . . *Sympathy.*
Throatwort . . . . *Neglected beauty.*
Thyme . . . . *Activity, or Courage.*
Tiger-flower . . . . *For once may pride befriend me.*
Traveler's Joy . . . . *Safety.*
Tree of Life . . . . *Old age.*
Trefoil . . . . *Revenge.*
Tremella Nestoc . . . . *Resistance.*
Trillium Pictum . . . . *Modest beauty.*
Triptilion Spinosum . . . . *Be prudent.*
Truffle . . . . *Surprise.*
Trumpet-flower . . . . *Fame.*
Tuberose . . . . *Dangerous pleasure.*
Tulip, Red . . . . *Declaration of love.*
Tulip, Variegated . . . . *Beautiful eyes.*
Tulip, Yellow . . . . *Hopeless love.*
Tulip . . . . *Charity.*
Tussilage, Sweet-scented . . . . *Justice shall be done you.*

Valerian . . . . *An accommodating disposition.*
Valerian, Greek . . . . *Rupture.*
Venice Sumach . . . . *Intellectual excellence. Splen-*
Venus's Car . . . . *Fly with me.*   [*dor.*
Venus's Looking-glass . . . . *Flattery.*
Venus's Trap . . . . *Deceit.*
Verbena, Pink . . . . *Family union.*
Verbena, Scarlet . . . . *Unite against evil.*
Verbena, White . . . . *Pray for me.*
Vernal-grass . . . . *Poor, but happy.*

Veronica . . . . *Fidelity.*
Veronica Speciosa. . . . . *Keep this for my sake.*
Vervain . . . . *Enchantment.*
Vine. . . . . *Intoxication.*
Violet, Blue . . . . *Faithfulness.*
Violet, Dame . . . . *Watchfulness.*
Violet, Sweet . . . . *Modesty.*
Violet, Yellow . . . . *Rural happiness. [and shade.*
Virginia Creeper . . . . *I cling to you both in sunshine*
Virginian Spiderwort . . . . *Momentary happiness.*
Virgin's Bower. . . . . *Filial love.*
Viscaria Oculata. . . . . *Will you dance with me?*
Volkamenia. . . . . *May you be happy.*

Wallflower . . . . *Fidelity in adversity.*
Walnut . . . . *Intellect. Stratagem.*
Watcher by the Wayside . . . . *Never Despair.*
Water-lily . . . . *Purity of heart.*
Watermelon . . . . *Bulkiness.*
Waxplant. . . . . *Susceptibility.*
Wheat-stalk . . . . *Riches.*
Whin . . . . *Anger.*
White Flytrap . . . . *Deceit.*
White Jasmine. . . . . *Amiableness.*
White Lily. . . . . *Purity and Modesty.*
White Mullein. . . . . *Good-nature.*
White Oak. . . . . *Independence.*
White Pink. . . . . *Talent.*
White Poplar. *Time.*
White Rose (dried) . . . . *Death preferable to loss of inno-*
Whortleberry . . . . *Treason.* [*cence.*
Willow, Creeping . . . . *Love forsaken.*
Willow, French . . . . *Bravery and humanity.*
Willow, Herb . . . . *Pretension.*
Willow, Water. . . . . *Freedom.*
Willow, Weeping . . . . *Mourning. Melancholy.*
Winter Cherry. . . . . *Deception.*
Wisteria . . . . *Welcome, fair stranger.*

Witch Hazel . . . . *A spell.*
Woodbine. . . . . *Fraternal love.*
Wood Sorrel . . . . *Joy. Maternal tenderness.*
Wormwood . . . . *Absence.*

Xanthium . . . . *Rudeness. Pertinacity.*
Xeranthemum . . . . *Cheerfulness under adversity.*

Yew . . . . *Sorrow. Cure for broken heart.*

Zephyr-flower . . . . *Expectation.*   *[love.*
Zinnia. . . . . *I mourn your absence. Lasting*

FLORAL POESY.

Flowers are love's truest language ; they betray,
  Like the divining rods of magi old,
  Where priceless wealth lies buried ; not of gold,
But love, strong love, that can never decay!
I send thee flowers, O dearest! and I deem
  That from their petals thou wilt hear sweet words,
  Whose music, clearer than the voice of birds,
When breathed to thee alone, perchance, may seem
All eloquent of feelings unexpressed.....*P. Benjamin.*

Flower. _____ *Sentiment.* _____

_____
_____
_____
_____
_____
_____
_____
_____
_____
_____
_____
_____
_____
_____
_____
_____
_____
_____
_____

AND impulses of deeper thought
Have come to me in solitude.

WORDSWORTH.

Flower. _____ *Sentiment.* _____

I LOVE thee ; yes, I feel
That on the fountain of my heart a seal
Is set, to keep its waters pure and bright
For thee.

SHELLEY.

Flower. _____ *Sentiment.* _____

_____
_____
_____
_____
_____
_____
_____
_____
_____
_____
_____
_____
_____
_____
_____
_____
_____
_____
_____
_____
_____

MUSIC! O, how faint, how weak,
Language fades before thy spell!
Why should feeling ever *speak*,
When thou canst breathe her soul so well?

MOORE.

Flower. _____ *Sentiment.* _____

LOVE'S soft sympathy imparts
That tender transport of delight
That beats in undivided hearts.

CARTWRIGHT.

Flower. _____ *Sentiment.* _____

BY day or night, in weal or woe,
That heart no longer free,
Must bear the love it cannot show,
And silent ache for thee.

BYRON.

FLORAL POESY.

DATE: _ /_ /_

Flower. _____ *Sentiment.* _____

_____

_____

_____

_____

_____

_____

_____

_____

_____

_____

_____

_____

_____

_____

_____

_____

_____

_____

_____

_____

_____

_____

THE air is full of poetry,— the air
Is living with its spirit ; and the waves
Dance to the music of its melodies,
And sparkle in its brightness.

PERCIVAL.

Flower. _____ *Sentiment.* _____

_____

_____

_____

_____

_____

_____

_____

_____

_____

_____

_____

_____

_____

_____

_____

_____

_____

_____

_____

_____

THOUGH changed from all that now thou art,
In shame, in sorrow, still thy heart
Would be the world to me, love.

L. E. LANDON

Flower. _____ *Sentiment.* _____

I SAW you every day, and all the day ;
And every day was still but as the first,
So eager was I still to see you more.

DRYDEN.

Flower. _____ *Sentiment.* _____

_____

_____

_____

_____

_____

_____

_____

_____

_____

_____

_____

_____

_____

_____

_____

_____

_____

_____

_____

_____

_____

TIME tempers love, but not removes,
More hallowed when its hope is fled ;
O, what are thousand living loves,
To that which cannot quit the dead?

BYRON.

Flower. _____ *Sentiment.* _____

'TIS like the spell of Hope's airy lay,
To whose sound through life we stray.

MOORE.

ACKNOWLEDGEMENTS,

AND PHOTO CREDITS.

M y grandmother, Sandra, cares for her flowers like friends— she inspires me to devote myself to even the most fragile things, to help them grow. Thank you for caring for me in the same way. To my family, thank you for believing in this project and enduring my long hours of speeches on the Victorian era and their fascination with the natural world, which has quickly become a fascination of my own.

PHOTO CREDITS: Thank you to the New York Public Library, Library of Congress, Biodiversity Heritage Library, The Smithsonian & many more libraries around the world for keeping gorgeous centuries-old illustrations accessible & available for viewing and use through Public Domain. All illustrations sourced through CC0 license unless otherwise listed below.

Edelweiss Illustration | Lemaris | Creative Market
Gerbera Daisy Illustration | DioFlow | Creative Market
Moonflower Illustration | Lusico2014 | Dreamstime

Special thanks to rawpixel for digitally enhancing many vintage botanical illustrations & to Tom Chalky and Heritage Type Co. for providing stunning antique design elements.

ABOUT THE POET,

OF 'HER HEART IS A WILDFLOWER' SERIES.

Rachel Clift is the author of a number of poetry & photography books including *to feel anything at all* and *to be remembered* from her ongoing 'Evolved Poetry' book series celebrating the changing of our seasons and the beauty of nature. She is also an artist and traveler, as shown in her books *your thoughts deserve a decent place to live* and *until we meet again* where readers are invited to explore the inner musings of her most heartfelt, vulnerable, and raw memories & self.

The 'Her Heart is a Wildflower' poems were originally written for brave women all over the world. This is the first & only time this collection of ten will be published to be read and enjoyed by you— to offer encouragement as you fill this book with your own poetry.

Based in the mountains of East Tennessee, Rachel spends her life surrounded and inspired by the magic of deep forests, winding rivers, and of course— endless wildflowers.

Follow @r.cliftpoetry on instagram and hashtag #thepoetryofwildflowers with your poems so I can read your words.
RCLIFTPOETRY.COM

INDEX.

by flower meaning & sentiment.

*A wildflower does not bloom because
it is told to do so— it blooms
because that is what
it was always meant to do.*

R. CLIFT.